Leaves Borrowed from Human Flesh

Also By Abigail Ardelle Zammit

Voices from the Land of Trees
(Middlesbrough: Smokestack, 2007)

Portrait of a Woman with Sea Urchin
(London: SPM Publications, 2015)

It has been said that the new frontier in poetry isn't discovering ways to experiment, nor is it finding strategies for preserving and honoring tradition. Instead, the most exciting work is actually bridging the gap between tradition and innovation. In other words, cultivating dialogue between postmodern techniques and inherited literary forms. This is one of the myriad ways that Abigail Ardelle Zammit's writerly craft excels. With incredible nuance and erudition, Zammit offers a feminist approach to meter that dazzles with its music, as well as its provocative intervention into the current discourse surrounding prosody. Zammit is a lavishly gifted writer, and this book is a formidable achievement.

—Kristina Marie Darling, Fulbright Scholar and author of
Daylight Has Already Come: Selected Poems

If you don't yet know Abigail Zammit's work, prepare yourself for the extraordinary. Her work is sensually evocative, highly energized and formally adventurous. The poems in *Leaves Borrowed from Human Flesh* are spatial and temporal adventures, from disciplined stanzas to free-form poems that explode into parallel texts and languages. They are inhabited by the actual and the mythical, by individual experience and collective memory. Some poems take on an evanescent counter presence, others re-purpose existing texts and redact them into a filigree of language within the dissolution of a black page. There is a powerful sense of human experience trying to be itself in the moment of sensory gestation whilst simultaneously haunted by history and the presence of other voices. This is a rich and dynamic collection, impossible to adequately sum up (or put down). Each poem re-defines the act of reading and the realization of multiple meanings.

—Graham Mort, *Black Shiver Moss*

Leaves Borrowed from Human Flesh is a richly dynamic collection, written out of Zammit's deeply felt commitment to poetry's potential for dialogue and eloquent silence alike. Sensuous, transformative and searching, it's a collection of exciting variety in its dramatizations of the spirits of place and the body, and of how the enduring past speaks to contemporary experience.

—Jane Draycott, *The Kingdom*

What an original, exacting poet! What a deeply rooted, tenderly blossoming voice! Each of Zammit's syllables springs forth with startling, necessary authenticity. In their lucent cherishing of the earth and hermetic composure, these surefooted poems place Abigail Zammit in the rare tradition of the daughters of H.D.

—Annie Finch,
Spells: New and Selected Poems

Abigail Ardelle Zammit is a shapeshifter, a traveller, a chronicler of far-flung places, ancient customs, songs of land and sea. In this new collection—perhaps her most ambitious—she plays with visual forms, ghazals, redactions, words scattered across the page as if a wind has blown them. She calls on the spirit of Daphne, through the filter of Ovid's *Metamorphosis,* and fashions for her a twenty-first century voice and resonance. Zammit never loses her lyrical power or precision—these are poems that both excite and haunt.

—Tamar Yoseloff,
A Formula for Night: New and Selected Poems

At once sensuous and violent, Abigail Ardelle Zammit's *Leaves Borrowed from Human Flesh* tells of the female body, of the body of the earth—their elemental transformations and plunderings. Her language is alchemic—poems as spells rise up from the page.

—Helen Ivory, *Constructing a Witch*

Spanning across geographies, contemporary politics, mythology, and attentive to the natural world as well as the glimmer and disquiet of love, Abigail Ardelle Zammit traverses the interior landscapes of ardor in poems as lyrically sharp as they are formally audacious. "Only death can leave me light," a woman pronounces from the underworld early in the book. Thus begins Zammit's *Leaves Borrowed from Human Flesh*—deathbound, seaswept and history-haunted, as a tribe prays to a flayed tree to grow back its branches; through the colonial delirium of settlers coaxing a "village of caged oaks and elms" in a foreign land; and through tributes—part-elegy, part-war cry—to a lineage of women, fearless and unruly. Above all, the peregrine speaker of these poems is always at home in the Other, open to transformation and awakening, in turn welcoming the reader to be changed.

—Rohan Chhetri, *Lost, Hurt, or in Transit Beautiful*

Leaves Borrowed from Human Flesh

Abigail Ardelle Zammit

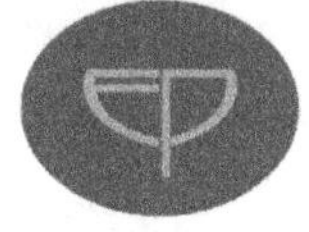

Etruscan Press
Wilkes University
84 West South Street
Wilkes-Barre, PA 18766
(570) 408-4546

Wilkes
University

www.etruscanpress.org

Published 2025 by Etruscan Press

Cover and interior design and typesetting by Lisa Reynolds
The text of this book is set in Adobe Garamond Pro.

First Edition

17 18 19 20 5 4 3 2 1

Library of Congress Cataloguing-in-Publication Data

Names: Zammit, Abigail A., 1976- author.
Title: Leaves borrowed from human flesh / Abigail Ardelle Zammit.
Description: First edition. | Wilkes-Barre, PA : Etruscan Press/Wilkes University, 2025. | Summary: "This collection offers a subversive take on poetic language, destabilizing the boundaries between genres, and shoving the confessional self off-centre"-- Provided by publisher.
Identifiers: LCCN 2024016872 | ISBN 9798988198574 (trade paperback)
Subjects: LCGFT: Poetry.
Classification: LCC PR9125.9.Z36 L43 2025 | DDC 811/.54--dc23/eng/20240418
LC record available at https://lccn.loc.gov/2024016872

Please turn to the back of this book for a list of the sustaining funders of Etruscan Press.

To my parents, whose love has nourished me throughout my life
and without whom my world would have been unutterable—

Table of Contents

I – Her Ears Flapping Gravely to the Beat of Human Voices

II – Her Body Was a Place She Called Home

III – Each Leaf Bears Its Own Red Map

And so it was we watched Zareb the elephant buffeting a canvas ball the size of a watermelon. One of his hind legs was tied to a chain that chimed whenever the old creature pushed the ball with its trunk. We could not leave. There was something terrible about the elephant's loneliness. It clung to him like moss, growing on his skin, sullying his ivory. The eyes had been broken into so many times, they could no longer see anything but the ball. All day long we watched as if suspended. And the minutes grew on us without warning until we were elephants, too, a mass of stone tethered to our bellies and our ears flapping gravely to the beat of human voices.

I – Her Ears Flapping Gravely to the Beat of Human Voices

Death by Water

After Guillén Pedemonti

There was the sea, impenitent,

the altar boys scuffling by the doorstep weighed
down by candelabra,

a man holding a stray oar, lance-like,
curious neighbors in feisty veils,

fishing nets splayed on walls
like scrambling roses,

and dawn, having tinged a rusty vine,
bearing a crucifix of light.

My ears—antlers carved from light

Tomb of a Roman woman, first half of 300 A.D.

I hear sobbing, the scrape of a spade,
the long cry of a chough. Lace-plated,
wrapped in ivory, my black hair grows
into wisps. I taste soil in my mouth,
lapis lazuli, then the thud of a stone—

they are laying me down.

Lapis manalis will close eyes, lips,
those softer parts which would not
yield to a husband's calloused hands
but spat a child's head, then another,
and another.

As they lay me down
they are chanting my name: *May earth be*
mild to you—in terra erit mitis—

Voconia Mecedonia.

Let no man visit me in the afterlife.
Neither my father, nor my father's father.
I will not rise into the flight of an egret,
nor will Horus guard me against evil.
If life has dealt me its scorpion blade,
only death can leave me light.

Way to Die

After "Ten Canoes"

He neither weeps nor calls his wives
but carries himself to his dance—

elbows bent, knotted fists, knotted
wrists. The camp-fire thrusts him

blue against the dusk, the silver trees,
the hammered blue of warrior blood—

fist and knee, fist and knee—warrior
whose hair will be clipped for the journey.

His soul trickles back to the water-pool—

light his body, lightened by death.
Ancestral spirits are waiting,

wakened with clapstick and didgeridoo,
crouched and taut, wakened with gum leaf

and song—the warriors stomping, leaping,
stomping, waterhole's a muddy silver.

His spirit's shrunken, laden with
leaf and bark, leaf and bark—Is there

no more water in this watering hole?

A Killing, Corazon de Madera[1]

Rio Negro, Armila

the medicine man said
awaken the wood with breath with fire
the spirit of the tree
dwells in each branch

but we heard a trickle in the foliage
gluttonous river
bearing traces of wave of tide
Rio Negro rooted in tree's trunk

ibe igua qirsu naba
naki asiswar

we grasped the machete
as if it were part of our longing

fearing caimans
nameless birds
dressed in night's electric blue

he said never sever the trunk
so we chopped it down

tree had traces of mud
salt-soul from the Pacific

igua ila nispero naki

we grasped the machete
as if it were part of our longing

ibe ila ila
sobga asiswar

a clean unwavering cut

---

1 Literally meaning 'the wood's heart,' which the natives would never remove. Instead, they cut some of the branches of the oldest trees to keep the wood for its healing and spiritual power, praying over it to awaken it. All italicized words refer to different types of trees in the Kuna language, spoken among the indigenous Kuna people of San Blas, Panama.

Transplanting a Landscape

Mount Wilson, Blue Mountains [2]

Do not ask of us
To be deserters, to disown our mother [...]
The gum cannot be trained into an oak.
—Oodgeroo Noonuccal

The trees hold up their arms—
women balancing thick canopies
of russets, wine—they feast on

falling, readying for wreaths
of snow, hollies ripening in May—
alien characters in aboriginal

dream-stories. Step closer—
phantoms wear white pinafores,
brown arms conjure bold laughter,

black eyes set on distant mists
where trunks are sparer and remnant
eucalypts luminous with silver.

Their songline is written in the loam,
in bole and bark, in the space they
give each other as they breathe—

trees that hold more sky than leaf
and branch. Yet I am here
in this village of caged oaks

and elms—a sycamore bows
cerise leaves towards a scarlet gate—
Somewhere, a black-eyed girl is

seized—the scourge of whiteness
taints her bloodline—
Her grandma's song is

in the caves, the basalt soil—
even the maples and cypresses
have heard—

---

[2] A township which became popular as a summer retreat for the wealthy in the latter part of the 19th century when extensive gardens were planted with English fruit trees, shrubs, plants, and other cool climate species that thrived among the remnant ferns and eucalypts.

Parroquia de San Jaime, Relleu

The spire is smothered in blue. In the niche,
a small Virgin wrapped in white, ribcage

pierced by the customary lance. If he could,
he'd beg the vine leaves, the gold-plated fields,

the ruined walls of the Moorish castle, each
stone, to enter, take comfort from the heat.

Siroccos lick stained windows
in those slow hours when he's just a man

in his green robe and an embroidered cross.
In his dreams, mountains will not speak—

The Hard Rules of Sea Water

After George Szirtes

You'll want it as god, as shoreline, as cornfield
swept by a breeze, until you discover
its propensity for wickedness, the lilt and swell

with which it handles human flesh,
cheeks bloated like rank waterlilies,
fingers meshed in luminous seaweed.

In the end, you too will slip sideways
over the bow, spot your liquid soul
in the sky's macula, hear the sea
spitting against what's left of you.

Ode to a Pound of Flesh

Summer Moon

Throw fear to the dog-stars, the bitch planets that slave at your day. Take the night, splitting yourself in halves, nibbled quarters. Neither white, nor withered, following me on the motorway—motionless, your godless eye on me in untamed speed, scattering darkness.

Carcinoma in situ

Let me take you for a field of ice, a moon-eyed fish, that piece of flesh they took from me to save me from myself—*papilloma*—palest butterfly, pupa-glued, your carnal spill. A year later, pupa moon *in situ*, a few cells short of——Christ didn't I want you out—zero C'd and silenced. Mad moon, they said, estrogen gravity—in it you shone—unwaxed, unwaned—never as whole as when you lay with me.

Goddess

Let no man set foot on you again. Salt is your desert's will—the O of want. Unwax. Unwane. Here—where it hurts, where human form
founders

II – Her Body Was a Place She Called Home

What Is It to Be the Blind Woman at the Helm

i

Sea slate-calm before sky
bursts into thunder—

Frogs sing the night—shoreline
teaming with coital frequencies—

leaping so fast you barely glimpse
their next coupling—I think of you

freighting your body from one
girl to the next, each name

surrendered to memory, and the
lies you told between pairings—

about love and how it sits with you,
as between a man and his scattered self—

ii

Today I spotted a striped vine snake
chewing a trembling frog, legs splayed

like a woman's. You came back to me
with the hum of betrayal

deep in your throat, and my own flesh
cleft like this river's—

On Discovering Her Refraction at a Sculpture Garden

After Guy Stevens

She's plaiting her hair by the stream—
her body's coracle floating upwards

towards the frescoed clouds
in their tapestry of light.

So much of one's self is about
positioning—

like this sculpture, full-bodied beam in marble
straight but slanting

aligned with the trees, the glade,
every falling leaf.

At the top of the stream it hums
like a tree quickening for spiked leaves.

Some would say *luster, splendor, delight*—

but underwater
there's more kelp than coral and conch.

She plaits her hair by the sea—
her sky bears tremors, scars, spiked refractions.

Ghazal/led

Write me if you will but **never** speak. The dream's demise
is tougher on the heart when tongue is **nettle**d with demise

A month ago, the studded blues and whites, the heal-all's seed—
you said *fidloqqom* with your eyes, then sang *starflowered with demise.*

Now **sext** me as you will **or** grieve me in this wisp of light.
De-**activate**'s my joy, though Facebook hasn't noticed our demise.

To love is not the same as fall in love and peacocks' eyes
are prayers stunned **in flight.** Who'll vouch each feather's sullied with demise?

No letterhead, nor signature to break the deal, **just** block and banish,
flee the bedroom scene. No friend of mine has bargained with demise.

Abīgayīl, now **thrash** the song **and** bid the psalmist ***tut!***
Before you know, dull-witted lust will have erased demise.

Do Early Blossoms Take Swift Leave?

Love's demise is stemmed in gold-leaf**,** curling stone,
unmarked graves and cankered grafts—whose mutinous leave?

Dare **no**t ponder Roman baths where once you kissed—
since he's gone, blight this heart with **bristly** leaves.

Never say "lover much missed," or coax dactylic **grief**.
Envious gods **will** gift to steal—so spurn-spit-leave!

Morph desire with quick release—"Go to, go **to**,"
still the mind—to think of him is still to leaf.

Acanthus watermarks each loss, each **ruin**ous shift.
Spear and tear all sighs and tears—say "Swift, woman, leave!"

Song

Armila, San Blas Islands

The sea goads its music into a storm.
No light in the bordering jungle
but the unrelenting call of cicadas,
the slipperiness of frogs, like

words, waking grass to a new green
somewhere beyond motif and mythic creature,
filling a salty river with tadpoles,
their wet crochets dancing one brief jig
before leaping away from a sea that is

never as turquoise as one wants it to be,
but gray-brown, turning purple with seaweed,
scavenging for buried signs, yearnings woven
from the not-so-blue of the sky.

The huts sealed inside their prayer,
but the sea's mouth salivates with howl,
makes a woman's hair turn mud-green in
one night so a man can reach far
inside her scalp looking for jade and silver.

She says the jungle has the wetness
of her tongue and she gives herself
completely. The man reaches for her
mouth. Thick foliage blocks the light.

Rodetes, Dama de Elche[3]

Omek Tannou. Ishtar. Astarte. Mother Tanit. *Virgo Caelestis*, Lady of the Sea, guarding the moon in the arch of your foot. The spheres unravelled their spools of water. Days when the ocean bruised your ears. Sea beds erupted like thunder breaking the still-born sky. Tides carried you to cliff-edged coves. Your gums turned to salt and your hands were rank seaweed. Eagles circled the sierras. Your cochleas sprouted sea shells, curled round your cheekbones. It is said on the Sabbath your ears filled with silt. Fledglings were picking each other's eyes, shrieks of survival ripping the skies. Then the blood came, red sand funnelling through the virgin womb. Sea-quakes birthed fires, furrowed flesh.

Omek Tannou. Ishtar. Astarte. Mother Tanit. *Virgo Caelestis*, Lady of the Sea, guarding the moon in the arch of your foot. A salt-less downpour swelling the earth. Rain drenched your tassels and intricate head-dress. Wheat sprouted overnight, husks falling at daybreak. It is said the faithful forced you into an oracle, brought you bread, white as the host. Your conch ears wore pigments of natural vermilion, tuned to the lash of each kill from the sky. In May they cremated their dead, pouring hot ashes in the arch of your back. Then they extracted your mollusc flesh, painted your skin in Egyptian blue. Your eyes were planets shedding their light, lips sealed against time, against fate, against prayer.

3 'Rodetes' are the large, wheel-like coils worn on each side of The Lady of Elche's face, a limestone bust discovered in 1897 at La Alcudia, Spain.

Two Landscapes, with Woman

For Daphne Caruana Galizia—
assassinated 16th October 2017.

i

Ólafsfjarðarvatn. Ice cracks beneath
my boots, fails to blot out the memory

of a woman, blasted—burnt pieces of
what she used to be

assembled for the autopsy.

There are crooks everywhere you look now.
The situation is desperate.
https://daphnecaruanagalizia.com/

ii

Firs in mutiny against the snow.

The cliff-edge ridged with steel blue,
outstretched hooves, rigor mortis.

It's the carcass of a sheep still woolly,
herbivorous cavity exposed.

Cavity: 'a hollow place, empty space in the body,'
1540s, from Middle French 'cavité,', from
Late Latin 'cavitatem,' 'hollowness,' from Latin
'cavus,' 'hollow.'

iii

I skate to ravens
cawing on each aerial.

Their beaks must reek
of fish gut. The crystal lake

conceals. Brings salt and herring,
then takes away. They say

to know all things, kill a raven—
cut out its heart, keep it

under the tongue—

Hrafn (Corvus corax) FUGLAMÁL
Vilji maður skilja fuglamal má drepa
hrafn skera úr honum hjartað og geyma I
munni sér undir tungunni.

Her Future Husband Appears to Her in the Shape of a Hawk

After Victoria Brookland

She never knows by which door
he enters, but suddenly
he is inside. Her red underdress
of hoops and holes stands stiff
as a lightning pole.
In her ribs, the flutter
of dying swifts.

She only knows his claws—
a memory of bruised lips,
her corset rupturing
into the pink of skinned hare.
No blood this time.
Each month wet feathers
line her uterus.

Little Red Riding Hood Goes Bushwalking

After "Into the Woods Red Riding Hood," sculpture at Scenic World

When wolf-man enters
her rainforest, the girl
slinks towards him
in a cloud of blush red,
letting him glimpse plump lips,
a half-formed breast.

She crouches at his feet,
red underskirt
shining crusted fur,
hood loosened
to blood-bark hair.

And he's leaning towards
her, man-fur knotted
with mistletoe, poison berry.
All the tree ferns are
screaming high trebles—
burls swirl into breasts.

The rainforest's closing him
in—tree-women armed
with pitchforks, pickaxes,
sharp twigs for his heart.
They're hacking his tongue.

House, Ayllú de Coyo

Atacama Desert

Two men talking about sex, drunk,
splattering words like spells—
They'll bring in the *curandero,*
the woman with fangs—

Somebody has given herself
prematurely. Somebody has fallen off
a swing. Somebody knows the timing's
almost always wrong—

And the dead are lining up
for counsel. Beyond the house,
the cordillera's red caves are
openings for wail and squall—

Women shudder, their mouths
erupt over tectonic plates, turning layers
of gypsum into arrowheads.
Men splatter words—

Voices spiraling
in the dusk. Somebody has fallen off
a swing. Somebody knows the timing's
almost always wrong—

The house, an oasis
of tattered starlight. Someone's flattening
the night for comfort. Someone burrows
its true darkness.

Seven Women in a Thatched Roof Hut

Armila Village

We come and go, our feet
heavy, electric. Toes stubbing
the dirt-floor, eyelids swollen with
mutinous fever. Night tears us
apart, its stars too close to be
borne, and the moon invisible
until the day we emerge from the river
carrying traces of our previous lives.

The thatched roof mutes our cries,
vomiting and weak in each other's arms,
then walking to the doctor's clinic—
ticking inside us, intravenous drips,
or the thud of a coconut splitting
open as it hits the ground. Back home, we
sleepwalk inside the locked hut, toes grimed,
sky-blue varnish peeling off our nails.

Someone is weeping. Someone sits
at the checkered window
eyeing dark men in army camouflage,
another sinks into the arms of a hammock.
Soot gathers in the folds of our bedclothes.
We've had too much ginger wine.
Someone is dreaming the ocean breath,
the frog's frenetic mating.

Inside us the moon is conceiving
strange shapes, a primordial beat,
a toddler carrying milk in a plastic cup.
And all this time we've been rummaging
through ourselves in the dark, our body's
engine almost stalling, wanting to walk
somewhere beyond the village,
the dirt, relentless, settling inside us.

The Ghosts of Punishment Island[4]

Unmarried girls who got pregnant were taken to Akampene and left to die.

All's muted except
the dip of paddles
fondling the water,
the woman's voice—
a lullaby sung
to the reeds.

Is it Akampene
she's heading for,
the thickening clouds
her guides, no longer
a mother with child,
but woman as hum,
as motion?

She's learned
each shiver of touch,
the hands given
and the lips withheld,
her body steered
further away.

Gray crowned cranes
watch from the grass.
She's gliding—lithe
through papyrus heads—
the land's

just a tapping point
from where she'll row
to those dead mothers
edging the lake.

---

4 BBC News, 27th April 2017

In This Shot, She Tears Herself from Her Treacherous Lover

After Jo Ann Callis's "Woman with Black Line"

She's kept the rattlebag of spite inside
her lungs—

a torch in a crowded mouth.

Only a black felt-line
parts the shining and knotty river

which arrows down to her spine.

Imagine the jolt—a firework
purpling into fuchsia.

Go on! Peel off her skin—

The truth's splayed on the sheet,
her torso facing the future.

Now, comb her hair—

Speak to Me

For Cristina, Athens, 31st December 2006

Little voice, speak—but not here, where crosses aren't for suicides—
sharply speak, as you did that last time when you said you were done with him.
Woman much missed, leap out of the bath before slitting your wrists—
death was a tear in a cloud—its entrails wreaths and chrysanthemums.

Rise like the mist beyond caves Paleolithic, slashing white stone,
claiming the air. Now shake away fears like raindrops and *call to me,*
call to me, goddess in flight, your season of madness gone—

No longer dying but coming—on campus, in public latrines,
his lust your command—"Pórni!" he called you, "Harlot! Poutàna!"
This is the heart he took, the tongue as far as the larynx.
Later, he ditched you. Sex as ash, but who could have warned you—

No longer coming, but dying. You were brief as a dragonfly—here's ocean,
the copper silicate of life as you craved it, sweet rot of your hair—
body still grazed like the stones that skimmed it—Say "Luck ran out—"

Have you not seen in the faltering light some sign of mystery,
rapture, delight?—this verse, your bold reach, the spiked line of your heart—
Sing then, little voice, sing! Come back as stone crop, snapdragon—
dog-headed and fierce—or acanthus, bear's breeches—hooded and wild—

body awakened to change—each bract, a scatter of sun—

heart

brief ly

seen

– hooded

sun

speak

This

line

as

body awake

Rise

Poutàna!

com brief dragonfly—

Woman

goddess

Harlot!

Sing sing!

slit

entrails

slash

public

tongue

ditch Sex

dragon

and bear

mad

coming

lust

verse

Come back as

—

The Fisherwoman's Revenge

He led six lives, each a different shade of crimson.

Every night she'd dream of slicing through his ponytail, not as one cuts hair or a beard, but as a fisherwoman slips a knife through a fish's guts. The intestine's dank seaweed.

"Love," he muttered in his sleep. She prepared to extract it from his mouth. The filaments shone in the near light. A tangled mass of sea-green.

III – Each Leaf Bears Its Own Red Map

Tree, Looming

After Van Gogh

A tree spikes free towards the sun,
vaster than the river,
the too lush green of the village
or the island cut out

like a gift—

It is not seed that it carries, nor that
swirl, the mass of a world
tipped on its axis   but a specter
singeing the sower   and his open hand—

Sonata: Valle de Marte

Desierto de Atacama

Ascent

Wind like hot rain, whipping
sand in your mouth. You're
a volcano, a copper mountain
sprouting from the rock-face, skin coated in
tourmaline, heart racing
backwards into a big bang, bacteria
exploding over the surface of a lake,
no days and no nights but
this blistered surface, the trickle of
sand solidifying, your womb
birthing a stone.

Panorama

The wind tatters the tin house
at the top of Valle de Marte.
You think of the Belgian missionary walking[5]
breathlessly to the throat of the valley,
quizzing his God.
What was it like for him
to believe in creation when dust
Catherine-wheeled into smoke,
rocks grew pitted and glazed,
bearing salt crystals that cracked
in the cooling sun?

---

5 Jesuit missionary Father Gustavo Le Paige

Descent

A stone is more than a stone—
there's salt in our mouths
as we kiss.

We're as lonely as the dogs
in San Pedro, meekly lifting our snouts
to be petted.

A beetle scrambles
down the dune in the hot hot sun,
the hot wind.

Perhaps time is a beetle
caught belly-up,
rolling off a cliff.

Variations on Hata Kamac

Trapped beneath the night-sky's hemorrhage,
stars raging with fires already spent,
lakes where petrified bacteria wait—
saltgrass sprouting from crevices of crusted sand,
cacti grazing the sky like words unhallowed,
haloed in light—
                                        Say, is this rain or ruin?
Storm-drops singe the air until we bleed.
All is temple-burn and tinnitus—
llamas penned in vain against huge sand-walls—
tenderness—the dust that comes from ruin.

Tenderness, the dust that came from ruin

Bodies penned in vain against the storm—
sex was temple-burn and tinnitus.
Dryness singed the air until we bled—
                                        Say, was it brume or ruin
haloed in light?
Cacti cursed the skies for piercing turquoise,
saltgrass split the bone that stalled decay,
lakes spewed life-forms brief as glowing phosphorus,
stars still raged with fires already spent—
trapped beneath the night-sky's hemorrhage,
lying low to scrounge another day—

Love, lie low to scrounge another breath

We're a hemorrhage of dust from ill-formed nebulae,
fires plumed with smoke when sparks collide,
brief the lake whose salt still holds us petrified,
sandstorms taunt each kiss that stalls decay.
Curse the sky that groaned for perfect turquoise,
fear thrashed us quicker than promised rain—
                                        Say, was it love that
borrowed light from ruin when
dryness singed the air until we bled—
dust, the tenderness that came from ruin,
or tenderness,
                    from rain that never   came—

Variations on Hata Kamac

Trapped beneath the night-sky's hemorrhage,
stars raging with **fire**s already spent,
lakes where petrified bacteria wait—
saltgrass sprouting from crevices of crusted sand,
cacti grazing the sky like words unhallowed,
haloed in light—
                    Say, is this rain or ruin?
Storm-drops singe the air until we bleed.
All is temple-burn and tinnitus—
llamas penned in vain against huge sand**-walls—**
tenderness—the dust that comes from ruin.

Tenderness, the dust that came from ruin

Bodies penned in vain against the storm—
sex was temple-burn and tinnitus.
Dryness singed the air until we bled—
                    Say, was it brume or ruin
haloed in light?
Cacti cursed the skies for piercing turquoise,
saltgrass **split the** bone that stalled decay,
lakes spewed life-forms brief as glowing phosphorus,
stars still raged with fires already spent—
trapped beneath the night-sky's hemorrhage,
lying low to scrounge another **day—**

Love, lie low to scrounge another breath

We're a hemorrhage of dust from ill-formed nebulae,
fires plumed with smoke when sparks collide,
brief the lake whose salt still holds us petrified,
sandstorms taunt each kiss that stalls decay.
Curse the sky that groaned for perfect turquoise,
fear thrashed us quick**er than** promised rain—
                    Say, was it love that
borrowed light from ruin when
dryness singed the air until we bled—
dust, the tenderness that came from ruin,
or tenderness,
          from rain that never   came—

against
light?
a hemorrhage

Variations on Hata Kamac

Trapped beneath the night-sky's hemorrhage;
stars raging with fires already spent;
lakes where petrified bacteria **wait—**
saltgrass sprouting from crevices of crusted sand;
cacti grazing the sky like words unhallowed,
haloed in light—
—————— Say, is this rain or ruin?
Storm-drops singe the air until we bleed.
All is temple-burn and tinnitus—
llamas penned in vain against huge sand-walls—
tenderness—the dust that comes from ruin.

Tender*ness, the dust that came from ruin*

Bodies penned in vain against the storm—
sex was temple-burn and tinnitus.
Dryness singed the air until we bled—
Say, **was** it brume or ruin
haloed in light?
Cacti cursed the skies for piercing turquoise;
saltgrass split the bone that stalled decay;
lakes spewed life-forms brief as glowing phosphorus;
stars still raged with fires already spent—
trapped beneath the night-sky's hemorrhage;
lying low to scrounge another day—

Love, lie low to scrounge another breath

We're a hemorrhage of dust from ill-formed nebulae,
fires plumed with smoke when sparks collide;
brief **the** lake whose salt still holds us petrified,
sandstorms taunt each kiss that stalls decay.
Curse the sky that groaned for perfect turquoise;
fear thrashed us quicker than promised **rain**—
Say, was it love that
borrowed light from ruin when
dryness singed the air until we bled—
dust, the tenderness that came from ruin,
or tenderness,
from rain that never came—

burn

ing low to

borrow

ruin

like

Bodies

that never came—

wait
in vain
brief
as a kiss

we penned
ruin
quicker
than love

spent
words
bled
to hemorrhage

we're
ill-formed bodies
huge like
stars

haloed
in phosphorus
to stall
—

Aria: on remaining ter-res-tri-al

The jeep carries us a-cross
sand dunes
cacti huge enough to remind us

guanacos raise delicate heads

Climb with me all the way

These are synonyms for want
distilled rain
icicle
wavelet
ripple-effect
vapor

Gravitational
can tear us a-
part
atom-ized

great expanse
yareta

there's water every-where

eyes made of dusk starlight

the deep
as-cent
up to where the sun is dying

melting crystal fractured pool
river-ing
space-ocean

inter-galactic

fields

Who'll bear witness?

bears?

In the Sea of Tranquility

Maria stretching

I don't want to be

hurtling

hydrogen colorless

eyes

tearing our heads

Everything starts with a bang

then

never forming but

Take this gift

Who

there was no water

sliding out of

our soul-waves

oyster onyx coral-in-agate

as your

nuclear fusion

from our feet

what?

trans forming

the glimpse of an after-birth

a jeep

words

stream-ed moon-scaped

stark

des-cent/d

air syll-a-ble

stretching the desert
fur-ther

Tropic of Capricorn

Ruta del Desierto, Chile

Dying Sun

By the roadside, *animitas* for the dead—a red truck, crushed bonnet intact, dashboard dust, the remains of human hair. Atacameños picnic on the highway to feed the departed—coca leaves, *chañar, rica-rica,* water from the salt lakes, then one last journey towards that southernmost point where the dead meet the sun—unaccompanied.

Even now when there are thirteen of us, we're always travelling alone, three four-wheelers daring the dirt road, this unreal replication of a film about a desert—the road empty save its dull orange hues, guanacos scattered round yellow bushes, the speckless blue of the sky, dunes threatening to devour us.

Moonscaped

Air's heavy and dry, clotting our nostrils, our eyes pink, grainy, half-open to unfamiliar darknesses where stars wink their reds and greens and the black spaces between the brightest points unspool the same note—how we're bound to crash into the thickest air, heavy-headed, our last trajectory, the Antarctic—like partygoers gathered in throngs, intoxicated, wandering into a lunar landscape, alone, spirits floating, laden with dust, with wind, with the memory of their own burial.

Across

We want words for this blankness where the body lags behind its shadow, our consciousness remote and animal-souled. Even when there's water, we carry unease wherever we go. The salt lagoons set their eyes on us—sharp turquoise, aqua—rivers struggle in the valleys between would-be orchards filled with figs, pomegranates, trees we cannot name.

We're merely replicas of ourselves molded into stone sculptures. Our voices flatten and die. The pampas are swelling with widgeon-weed, but we're barely breathing, each huff a step towards that invisible border. The dreaded puna tugs at our lungs, and all's gone but one red truck by the roadside, this lone fox nudging our bones.

The Tree Answers Back

The tree leans its sturdy body over the ocean
and I ask of it what it might mean
to be other than oneself—Each heart-leaf bears
its own red map—the just-unfurled,
the brightest emerald, the already fallen—

"Tree, how do you hold yourself over
the water, so whole, almost unmoved,
your reflection as fleeting as the passing
of this cloud, this woman, hatless
and falling for every little thing—a seashell,
the broken husk of a sea-urchin,
someone wading further away?"

On Not Seeing the Evening Lights
Ólafsfjörður, 2019

We heard the ocean's full gallop,
ice crashed from the eaves,
snow blasted at windows,
the minutest crevices made light
of our sorrows, long hours of gusts
blowing us out of ourselves—
we floated above the tundra,
or lay low, vegetative, learning
the stunted growth of Icelandic trees.

Every night now, we're sniffing
auroras, prickly air, solar ejections
fizzing earth's magnetic shields.
Night sky teases with forms
indistinguishable from clouds.
We say "Yes! Yes!" but no longer
trust our eyes. When we walk back,
toes beckoning for warmth, a sword-
flash behind us, too quick to be seen.

Tourists, despite ourselves, wanting
luminous green, the long exposure
that makes everything visible,
ignorant of how long it takes
to know light from light.
We're exhausted polar bears
drifting on ice floes. Inside us,
the squeak of snow deepens—

We drink whisky to Moreno—

i

still growing as steadily
as it is melting. Slow,

reticent, the glacier's tear—
acutest blue from its core.

We're looking deep for ultraviolet,
the reflected melt of light.

Inside us there is too
this gentle dissolution—

ii

So in dreams, a glacier re-forms
out of the cold of melt and muck.

Sapphire crystals battle the water.
We catch the brightness of reflected light,

witness how it is to walk out of sleep
into a world of drifting ice.

Fractured Pagoda[6]

Coal mining subsidence, Ben Bullen State Forest

Strange thunder sinks
too deep.

A small creek is giving up its
ghost—browning moss,

dead snails, a water dragon
stretched out on a stone.

Once my ripped half
plummets down,

will I still be here,
piqued by lightning

from a wanton sky?

---

6 Pagodas are cone-shaped, smooth, or platy sandstone formations in the Northwestern Blue Mountains region, Australia. They were laid down in a massive river delta some 250 million years ago and are now threatened by mining.

Rain, Uganda

Like me who have no love which this wild rain
Has not dissolved . . .
—Edward Thomas, "Rain"

The traveler's tree at your window
collects rain water, fruitless and fan-like.
It gives nothing away. Wants nothing
but rain to feed it so it can grow
taller than the houses with their perfect rooftops.

And you ask if it's wrong to be like this—
your body visited by rain—
to *be* the rain, wanting torrent and flood
and nothing else. Nothing that the world
has failed to gift you.

Bush Diary

Cathedral Canyon, Wollemi National Park

i

You've nothing left
but your body, the bush,
the sandstone—

nothing could exceed in dreariness
the appearance of the tracks through
which we journeyed—[7]

Nothing's left of love
or deceit—you're not
unhinged by mothering,
by disease—

our advance and our retreat
were alike cut off—

Far from the campsite where families
play ball, their white caravans
curbing the wild—

ii

Scratch your arms against
the swords of grass trees,
white-tipped warriors

lancing the air,
coral ferns splitting

air heavy, sky dull

unexpectedly,
bullet ants like questions

How could an European

flies exceedingly troublesome

asked of the body—

expect to find food?

Branches raise themselves

trees stunted,
unfit for building

from inclined trees,
the alchemy of sunlight
and dying moth—
all species arrayed,
disarrayed.

The aspect of the country beneath them
much disappointed the travellers.

iii

Those first Europeans searching
for versions of home
suffered this ghost-gray tinge
that mutes the landscape—

the most brilliant silvery lustre

everything singular, unknown.

At dusk, life would lapse into
another form, gum trees silvering
the last light, a vision so unlike
anything they'd seen,

the country, exceedingly broken and confused

they were lost, disarrayed—

iv

Slip on gum leaf and moss
aiming for the promised caves, the story

we passed hollow
after hollow

beyond the story—questions
you never know the answer to—

no view of distant objects

the spirit, detached from the body,
becomes shape and form,

like these secret openings in the rock,
millennia of crumbling, finest sands

no smoke to betray
a water hole

in cream and gold, each ledge
melting into another.

v

Caves whose hues break
into waves, rusts,
terracottas, grooves
oranging into belief—
bright ambers, pale pinks,
the reds of lichens
dotting the rock-face,

however unfit for civilized man
it seemed a most desirable one
for the savage

ironstone staining
your hand—

vi

You're still here, there,
adjusting lens, tripod,

failing to frame the whole, *the horizon unbroken*
until tired, disarrayed,
no glittering light

among the trees you put everything away,
walk towards the interior—

down below, three angophoras
ringed in light, a eucalypt
flowering out of season— *baffled in every instance*

7 All marginal quotes are taken from 19th century *Journals of Inland Exploration* which may be found at The University of Sydney's library database.

Earth, Wake One Heart

The body scatters, all hematite and song—
Lichen retreat, bleached tendrils all we've got. [fledged lichen]
A redstart came to visit, but not for long. [tidal

tail] Taste blood and ore once wistfulness takes hold— [him/hymn]
Love wakes him not enough, his heart's too taut.
The body's scatter is hematite and song. [blotting
field]

Beak-to-beak, not knowing telluride from gold,
we sought to sprawl our seconds, stay the rot— [rusty beak]
[skeletal shoreline] Two redstarts came to visit, but not for long.

If feathers swarm the house, the threshold's gone.
Take note, old heart—each rusty tail a clot.
Scattered bodies are hematite and song. [sprawling

heart]
Aged redstarts sing of tides that wane [blood song]— along
the shoreline, each skeleton's a soggy blot—
Some fledglings come to visit, but not for long. [bleached bodies]

Lovers retreat, and grief is all we've borne— [hem/hymn]
Allot each loss to quantum fields gone naught.
[grieve— say quantum grief…]
Our bodies scattered—all hematite and song—
When redstarts come to visit, it's never for long.

[Scatter, old heart

——

[fledged lichen]
[tidal

tail] [him/hymn]

[blotting
field]

[rusty beak]
[skeletal shoreline]

[sprawling

heart]
[blood song]

[bleached bodies]

[hem/hymn]

[grieve— say quantum grief…]

[Scatter, old heart
—

My B o d y is a Room with Shadows
dan ġismi kamra dellijiet

(i) *hand*—

speak sorrow in your mother tongue—
let the sixth vowel
the long-lying 'ie' cleat you to
my clavicle
your heart/hurt trochaic with lust/love

do not leave before you've entered/plundered

in openness I let you go / (please come back)

this is you climbing out of the light (nightjar: too used to darkness)

both of us exiting (are we hieroglyphs then?)

kienu *mietu*

they died—exiting—

extinction from *'extinguere'*

razed flesh—this is erasure

(there is no mustard tree here)
(the pines have withdrawn)

wake to sorrow

I must pine like the maiden
whose hand became a taper
for light to shine through

(say grief's a ballad)

was it fire wiped out the mustard seed
or were we agents too

caricatures in a flaming landscape—

my mouth ghosting your voice

your b o d y—silting/citing the
shadows—

(ii) *navel*—

don’t tell me when you peeled off the skin all you found
was the meat of us

hunger came to you first

before I made you you were the ripped mouth of a cypress cone

you came because I called you
alone in the fluorescent blue
of a viral landscape
the mycelial edge of dawn I conjured your contours

stretching my anemonal pulp to meet you
nuzzling the scalding tip of your snow

you came after closure the year's end pluming
with promise / but weren't you already here?

I knew you by the numb scent of asphodel

yes you taught me sex through
language

gorging on dopamine serotonin

toxic / in-to-xi-ca-ting

Was it you that I loved or what I made of you?

don't tell me it's the same

IV – Leaves Borrowed from Human Flesh

#wearedaphne

Erasures of Ovid's *Metamorphoses*

From the prose translations by Mary M. Innes
(U.K.: Penguin Random House, 1955).

Where there is despair, let me profit from it;
where there is darkness, let me give it a banking license.

Running Commentary, Daphne Caruana Galizia's Notebook,
May 12th 2017, 3:45 a.m.

Running Commentary, Daphne Caruana Galizia's Notebook
From _Metamorphoses, Book III,_ Echo and Narcissus

that talkative nymph who cannot stay silent

always answers back.
still a body then, not just a voice: she was
always chattering, her power of speech
to repeat the many phrases
she heard.

knowing well what she did, endless

the powers of that tongue

she

followed secretly The more
closely she followed, the nearer the fire which scorched her:

"Here!"

"Come!"

words echoed back.

anxious thoughts kept her awake,

till finally her voice alone remained; her bones, they say, were turned to stone.

heard by all: her voice still lives.

"17 Black—Dubai," *Running Commentary*, February 22nd 2017, 6:43 p.m.
From *Metamorphoses, Book IV,* Salmacis and Hermaphroditus

thinking himself unobserved alone,
he

could scarcely bear to
wait,

she held
him

in spite of all his efforts to slip from her grasp, she twined around
him

like the ivy
encircling tall tree trunks,

You may fight, you rogue, but you will not escape.

the day was ended,
the hour was approaching
neither daylight nor darkness,
the night
almost come.

16th October 2017, 2:45 p.m.

From *Metamorphoses, Book 1,* The Transformation of Daphne

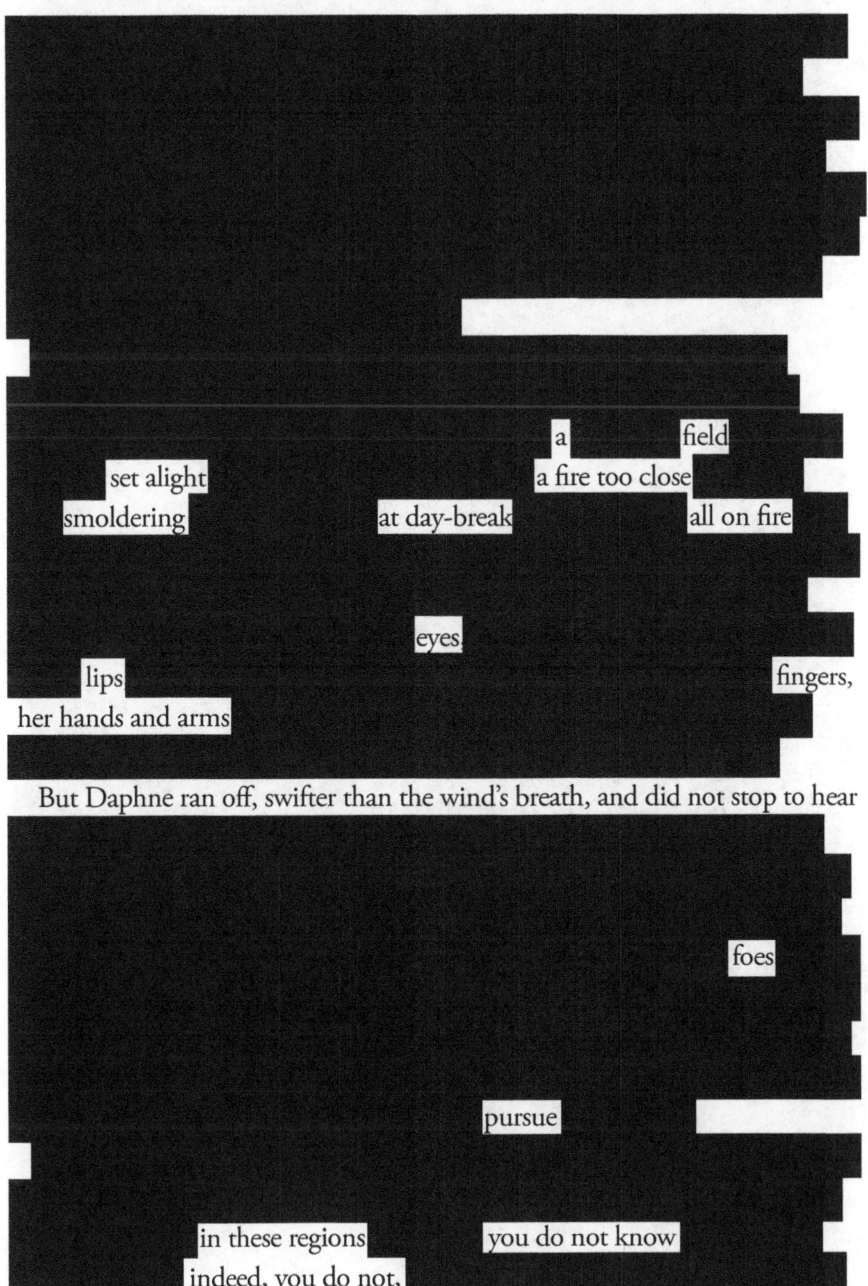

a field
set alight a fire too close
smoldering at day-break all on fire

eyes
lips fingers,
her hands and arms

But Daphne ran off, swifter than the wind's breath, and did not stop to hear

foes

pursue

in these regions you do not know
indeed, you do not,

the past, the present, the future

All

hers

words unfinished;

follow close

some transformation,

her heart still beating under the new bark.

long processions, voices raise the song
Augustus' gateposts
the wreath of oak leaves that will hang
there
at all times

"When hell broke loose," *Malta Today*, 18th October 2017.
From *Metamorphoses, Book VI,* The Lycian Peasants

The story is not well-known,

threatening
heaping insults
they stirred up
pure malice
their foul tongues still kept up their
bickering,
Their voices became harsher,
their ill-natured croakings stretched their gaping mouths
wider.

"There are crooks everywhere you look," *Running Commentary*, 16th October 2017, 14:35.

From *Metamorphoses, Book VI,* Procne, Tereus and Philomela

excited by his own
passionate nature, for the people of his country are an emotional race
he burned
His impulse was to bribe to
undermine to tempt

He was impatient

enforced his arguments

The very acts which furthered
his scheme made people believe he was devoted
he was praised for his criminal behaviour.

the sun had but little way to go

scoundrel! Are you quite unmoved

? Do you care nothing

one day no matter when, you will pay the penalty

proclaim your deeds

to the dark earth.

Even after this atrocity

the body mutilated.

he had the audacity to go back

told a

tale of his own invention

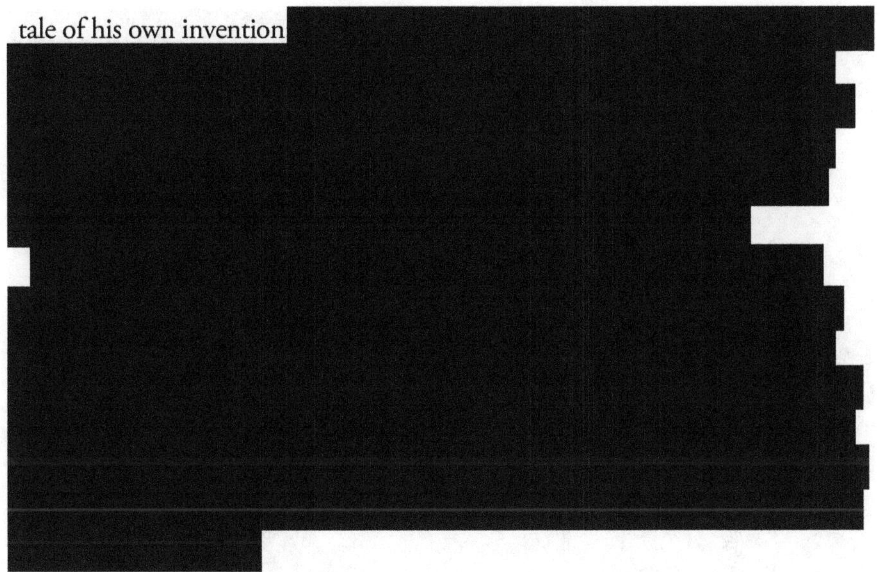

"Malta Murder Investigation Closes In on 'Mafia State'," *The New York Times,* 19th December 2019.

From *Metamorphoses, Book VIII,* Scylla and Minos

But surely every man is his own god:

'Where are you going?
Where are
you off to, hard-hearted
My own country
betrayed

"U l-kotra qamet f'daqqa"[8]

From *Metamorphoses, Book III,* Pentheus Scorns the Prophet

The whole populace streamed out men and women, old and young

cymbals clashing,

trumpets,

wailing women and tinkling tambourines,

show spirit

bring down walls

we should be free

no need for concealment

drag that leader here in chains. Waste no time

8 "And the people rose in unison," from "Jum ir-Rebħ," by the poet Rużar Briffa. This well-known poem was inspired by a football match which took place in 1945; the King's Own Band failed to play the Maltese national anthem before the game's commencement, but the Maltese spectators rose to sing it anyway.

Melita, November 2019

From *Metamorphoses, Book I,* The Crimes of Men and Giants

cancer incurable, the healthy
part infected.

"No stone unturned," Public Inquiry Ongoing, December 2020.
From *Metamorphoses, Book VIII,* The Cretan Labyrinth

devious paths winding
this way
and that,
countless
wandering paths

but
the sky, surely, is open

"Nobody deserves to die," *Malta Today*, 18th October 2017.
From *Metamorphoses, Book XI*, Ceyx and Alcyone

Sleep, where the sun's rays
can never reach,
no anxious dogs
break the silence,
no sound of branches swaying in the wind, or harsh
quarrelling of human tongues. Voiceless quiet
over the dark earth.

Invicta

From *Metamorphoses, Book XV,* The Philosophy of Pythagoras

why are you terrified by

shadows and empty names

?

All things change,

but nothing dies

Therefore, in case family

feeling prove less strong than greedy appetite,

do not nourish

blood with blood.

Everything

in a state of flux

don't you see the year passing
what
we have been,
we shall not be to-morrow.

one shape from another
begin
to be something different

return as a mighty river
pour forth water

“Your pen has been silenced but your voice will live on,” *The Malta Independent*, 19th October 2017.

From *Metamorphoses, Book IX,* Byblis and Caunus

follow the example
no regard for reputation or fear of
scandal
fill the tablets
add the last line in the margin
seal the story

#stillwearedaphne

I tell and retell the story / to find the answer [9]

Part Two: Erasures of Ovid's *Metamorphoses*

From *The Metamorphoses of Ovid: A New Verse Translation by Allen Mandelbaum* (San Diego: Harcourt, Inc., 1993).

1. From *Dryope, Book IX*

Change form sister—
tear against fate—
disturb the blossom of blood—
stay like roots within the ground,
climb slowly from below and gradually cover all.

Dearest sister,
I brought all my strength to seek warm wood,
leaves that sprout from your body.

Voice plays beneath these branches:
here—within this trunk—
lean towards my lips
let life and speech, new-made
transform.

2. From *Pyramus and Thisbe, Book IV*

Within the mighty city ringed by walls—
one thin crack no one had seen;
you were the first to find it,

---

9 H.D., *Helen in Egypt*, Book 6, 4 (New York: New Directions, 1974).

made that cleft a passageway for whispers:
words stretched wide enough to reach the sky.

Watch the city beneath a tree—
she sits with trembling feet;
by night bloody tatters
underneath the shady tree.
Blood sends out a hissing stream.
Tree's fruits bloodstained;
the tree's familiar shape laments her name—
boughs shade one wretched body,
words still warm.

3. From *Apollo and Daphne, Book I*

River, wild beasts—
all earthly things kindle love
but the god of oracles reads the future wrongly.
He can't imagine the lamb, the trembling dove
crossing trackless places.

Too rash, no herb to heal its master,
he races on, almost sure he's won—
his mouth escapes his jaws.
All that is left is crown, portal, bough—

4. From *Myrrha & Cinyras, Book X*

Why do I keep
coming back?
names, signs
hid beneath
her words: the fire
that feeds
the massive trunk

blows this way,
then that.

—But, come,
break loose
voice—
warn, probe,
draw closer—
name guilt in speech,
cross open fields—
transform her marrow,
her blood to sap;

and tree
envelop
her breasts—
she will be
remembered.
Come forth words;
trunk bends and
moans; boughs
speak, deliver
body to form.

Daphne: five ways in which to burn

(for lust)

How's a woman ever ready?

these limbs which root me to the ground when I would

(for glory)

Bind fast each branch. Seal. Kneel. Beseech.

This is no wreath —————— Augustus, old fool!

Ask the sacred reef. Ask Pliny the Elder.

Yes, ask Pythia—

“Who’s the woman who’ll set the sea on fire?”

(for truth)

She said: *burn no incense for the gods. When have they ever loved you back?*

Yes, send back those liars, the poets.

My heart has spoken thus: ________________

What of words? What of asphodels scavenged by moonlight?

(I'd have vouched their pink lids were a warning)

(for speech)

What if each leaf were borrowed from human flesh?

trunk as womb   as lightning bolt   as jagged   signal

What does the tree already know?

Old fool!
Has exile ever sealed the story?

(for spells)

Laurel forests slow to leaf

slow to leaf

"What burns but does not die?"

ACKNOWLEDGMENTS

From *Metamorphosis* by Ovid, translated by Mary M. Innes, published by Penguin Classics. Reprinted by permission of Penguin Books Limited.

From "Dryope" (Book IX), "Pyramus & Thisbe" (Book IV), "Apollo and Daphne" (Book I), "Myrrha & Cinyras" (Book X) from *The Metamorphoses of Ovid: A New Verse Translation* by Allen Mandelbaum. Copyright©1993 by Allen Mendelbaum. Used by permission of HarperCollins Publishers.

With deep gratefulness to the editors of the following journals for publishing earlier versions of these poems:

Introductory prose poem, "My ears—antlers carved from light," *Pratik: A Magazine of Contemporary Writing,* Summer/Fall 2018.

"Death by Water," *The Ekphrastic Review,* 24th March 2018.

"A Killing, Corazon de Madera" was a finalist in the 2022 Montreal International Poetry Competition and has been published in the *The Montreal Poetry Prize Anthology 2022,* Ed. MacLaren, Eli, (Montreal: Véhicule Press, 2023).

"Ode to a Pound of Flesh," *Gutter,* Issue 24.

"On Discovering Her Refraction at a Sculpture Garden," *Sarasvati,* Issue 067 & 068, December-February 2022/23.

"Song," *The High Window,* 2020.

"Rodetes, Dama de Elche," *O:JA&L,* 26th November 2020.

"Two Landscapes, with Woman," *Modern Poetry in Translation,* "Call the Sea a Poet: Focus on Malta," No. 2, 2023.

"Her Future Husband Appears to Her in the Shape of a Hawk" and "House, Ayllú de Coyo," *Ink Sweat and Tears,* 5th June 2020 and 1st

December 2022.

"Seven Women in a Thatched Rood Hut," "Tropic of Capricorn," "We Drink Whisky to Moreno—," *Natural Bridge, Boulevard,* 2021.

"In This Shot, She Tears Herself from Her Treacherous Lover," *The Ofi Press;* Issue 67.

"Speak to Me," "Bush Diary," "My Body Is a Room with Shadows," *The Tupelo Quarterly,* Issue 27.

#wearedaphne, *The Tupelo Quarterly,* Issue 25.

"Daphne: five ways in which to burn," *The Tupelo Quarterly,* Issue 30.

A poetry book is never solely the work of a single person, which is why I would like to thank everyone at Etruscan Press for putting so much faith in my work, particularly Amanda Rabaduex and Philip Brady. A big thank you to Pamela Turchin for her patience with the manuscript's evolution. Thanks to Lisa Reynolds for setting poem to page. I am eternally grateful to all those poets, tutors and editors who have offered advice on the poems in this collection, especially to Kristina Marie Darling and Jeffrey Levine for their invaluable feedback and unwavering support. Heartfelt thanks to Lucia Boldrini for championing my work. Love to Annie Finch for the magic of metrical knowledge. I owe my mother, father, sister and closest friends more than a poem can ever express—thank you for always listening. For always believing. May there always be light in your lives.

About the Author

Abigail Ardelle Zammit is a Maltese writer and the author of two poetry collections, *Voices from the Land of Trees* (Middlesbrough: Smokestack, 2007) and *Portrait of a Woman with Sea Urchin* (London: Sentinel, 2015), which won second prize in the SPM Poetry Competition. Her poetry and reviews have been published in international journals including *Matter, Tupelo Quarterly, Boulevard, Gutter, Modern Poetry in Translation, Mslexia, Poetry International, The SHOp, Iota, Aesthetica, Ink Sweat and Tears,* and *The Ekphrastic Review.* She has co-authored two Maltese-English poetry pamphlets and written a Seamus Heaney guidebook for post-secondary students. Her most recent manuscripts have been shortlisted for the Cinnamon Press Literature Award 2022, the Tupelo Press Open Reading Period 2022, the 2023 Sunken Garden Poetry Chapbook Prize and the 2023 Snowbound Chapbook Award. Zammit's passion for on-site research has allowed her to take part in artistic residencies around four continents.

Books from Etruscan Press

Zarathustra Must Die | Dorian Alexander
The Disappearance of Seth | Kazim Ali
The Last Orgasm | Nin Andrews
Drift Ice | Jennifer Atkinson
Crow Man | Tom Bailey
Coronology | Claire Bateman
Viscera | Felice Belle
Reading the Signs and other itinerant essays | Stephen Benz
Topographies | Stephen Benz
What We Ask of Flesh | Remica L. Bingham
The Greatest Jewish-American Lover in Hungarian History | Michael Blumenthal
No Hurry | Michael Blumenthal
Choir of the Wells | Bruce Bond
Cinder | Bruce Bond
The Other Sky | Bruce Bond and Aron Wiesenfeld
Peal | Bruce Bond
Scar | Bruce Bond
Until We Talk | Darrell Bourque and Bill Gingles
Big Time | Rus Bradburd
Poems and Their Making: A Conversation | Moderated by Philip Brady
Crave: Sojourn of a Hungry Soul | Laurie Jean Cannady
Toucans in the Arctic | Scott Coffel
Sixteen | Auguste Corteau
Don't Mind Me | Brian Coughlan
Wattle & Daub | Brian Coughlan
Body of a Dancer | Renée E. D'Aoust
Generations: Lullaby with Incendiary Device, The Nazi Patrol, and How It Is That We | Dante Di Stefano, William Heyen, and H. L. Hix
Ill Angels | Dante Di Stefano
Aard-vark to Axolotl: Pictures From my Grandfather's Dictionary | Karen Donovan
Trio: Planet Parable, Run: A Verse-History of Victoria Woodhull, and Endless Body | Karen Donovan, Diane Raptosh, and Daneen Wardrop
Scything Grace | Sean Thomas Dougherty
Areas of Fog | Will Dowd
Romer | Robert Eastwood
Wait for God to Notice | Sari Fordham
Bon Courage: Essays on Inheritance, Citizenship, and a Creative Life | Ru Freeman
Surrendering Oz | Bonnie Friedman
Funeral Playlist | Sarah Gorham

Nahoonkara | Peter Grandbois
Triptych: The Three-Legged World, In Time, and Orpheus & Echo | Peter Grandbois, James McCorkle, and Robert Miltner
The Candle: Poems of Our 20th Century Holocausts | William Heyen
The Confessions of Doc Williams & Other Poems | William Heyen
The Football Corporations | William Heyen
A Poetics of Hiroshima | William Heyen
September 11, 2001: American Writers Respond | Edited by William Heyen
Shoah Train | William Heyen
American Anger: An Evidentiary | H. L. Hix
As Easy As Lying | H. L. Hix
As Much As, If Not More Than | H. L. Hix
Chromatic | H. L. Hix
Demonstrategy: Poetry, For and Against | H. L. Hix
First Fire, Then Birds | H. L. Hix
God Bless | H. L. Hix
I'm Here to Learn to Dream in Your Language | H. L. Hix
Incident Light | H. L. Hix
Legible Heavens | H. L. Hix
Lines of Inquiry | H. L. Hix
Rain Inscription | H. L. Hix
Shadows of Houses | H. L. Hix
Wild and Whirling Words: A Poetic Conversation | Moderated by H. L. Hix
All the Difference | Patricia Horvath
Art Into Life | Frederick R. Karl
Free Concert: New and Selected Poems | Milton Kessler
Who's Afraid of Helen of Troy: An Essay on Love | David Lazar
Black Metamorphoses | Shanta Lee
Mailer's Last Days: New and Selected Remembrances of a Life in Literature | J. Michael Lennon
Parallel Lives | Michael Lind
The Burning House | Paul Lisicky
Museum of Stones | Lynn Lurie
Quick Kills | Lynn Lurie
Synergos | Roberto Manzano
The Gambler's Nephew | Jack Matthews
American Mother | Colum McCann with Diane Foley
The Subtle Bodies | James McCorkle
An Archaeology of Yearning | Bruce Mills
Arcadia Road: A Trilogy | Thorpe Moeckel
Venison | Thorpe Moeckel
So Late, So Soon | Carol Moldaw

The Widening | Carol Moldaw
Clay and Star: Selected Poems of Liliana Ursu | Translated by Mihaela Moscaliuc
Cannot Stay: Essays on Travel | Kevin Oderman
White Vespa | Kevin Oderman
Also Dark | Angelique Palmer
Fates: The Medea Notebooks, Starfish Wash-Up, and overflow of an unknown self |
Ann Pedone, Katherine Soniat, and D. M. Spitzer
The Dog Looks Happy Upside Down | Meg Pokrass
Mr. Either/Or | Aaron Poochigian
Mr. Either/Or : All the Rage | Aaron Poochigian
The Shyster's Daughter | Paula Priamos
Help Wanted: Female | Sara Pritchard
American Amnesiac | Diane Raptosh
Dear Z: The Zygote Epistles | Diane Raptosh
Human Directional | Diane Raptosh
I Eric America | Diane Raptosh
50 Miles | Sheryl St. Germain
Saint Joe's Passion | J.D. Schraffenberger
Lies Will Take You Somewhere | Sheila Schwartz
Fast Animal | Tim Seibles
One Turn Around the Sun | Tim Seibles
Voodoo Libretto: New and Selected Poems | Tim Seibles
Rough Ground | Alix Anne Shaw
A Heaven Wrought of Iron: Poems From the Odyssey | D. M. Spitzer
American Fugue | Alexis Stamatis
Variations in the Key of K | Alex Stein
The Casanova Chronicles | Myrna Stone
Luz Bones | Myrna Stone
In the Cemetery of the Orange Trees | Jeff Talarigo
The White Horse: A Colombian Journey | Diane Thiel
The Arsonist's Song Has Nothing to Do With Fire | Allison Titus
Bestiality of the Involved | Spring Ulmer
The Waw | Jacqueline Gay Walley
Silk Road | Daneen Wardrop
Sinnerman | Michael Waters
The Fugitive Self | John Wheatcroft
YOU. | Joseph P. Wood

Etruscan Press Is Proud of Support Received From

Wilkes University

Wilkes University

Ohio Arts Council

The Stephen & Jeryl Oristaglio Foundation

Community of Literary Magazines and Presses

National Endowment for the Arts

Drs. Barbara Brothers & Gratia Murphy Endowment

Founded in 2001 with a generous grant from the Oristaglio Foundation, Etruscan Press is a nonprofit cooperative of poets and writers working to produce and promote books that nurture the dialogue among genres, achieve a distinctive voice, and reshape the literary and cultural histories of which we are a part.

www.etruscanpress.org
Etruscan Press books may be ordered from

Consortium Book Sales and Distribution
800.283.3572
www.cbsd.com

Etruscan Press is a 501(c)(3) nonprofit organization.
Contributions to Etruscan Press are tax deductible
as allowed under applicable law.
For more information, a prospectus,
or to order one of our titles,
contact us at books@etruscanpress.org.

www.ingramcontent.com/pod-product-compliance
Lightning Source LLC
Jackson TN
JSHW022027200225
79214JS00001B/4

9798988198574